Reading

POST

Images of

Reading

and surrounding villages

Reading
POST

Images of
Reading
and surrounding villages

H A R O L D   H I L L

Breedon Books
Publishing Company
Derby

First published in Great Britain by
The Breedon Books Publishing Company Limited
44 Friar Gate, Derby, DE1 1DA
1995

Acknowledgements

My sincere thanks to the following people who have loaned me
pictures or allowed the use of them:

The Reading Reference Library
Friths Pictures
Mr Douglas Noyes
The Reading Evening Post

A special thanks to Miss Cheryl Clarke for her devoted help in the
preparation of this book, without which it would not have been
possible.

ISBN 1 85983 024 2

Printed and bound by Butler & Tanner, Frome, Somerset
Covers printed by Premier Print, Nottingham.
Colour separations by Colour Services, Leicester.

Contents

Introduction

THIS is a look at the ancient town of Reading over the last 150 years and it is difficult to give an introduction without delving into the history of the town from the days of the Abbey. But I will decline from this because I feel the last 150 years have been so exciting in the development of the town and, indeed, the area surrounding Reading that it is important to concentrate on that.

I must first, however, mention an original staple industry of Reading from the 17th century. This was the cloth trade which was the mainstay of the town for a time. This trade was mainly based around an area of the town of Minster Street and Gun Street known as The Oracle.

The industry was started in 1624 by a London clothier called John Kendrick who was originally a native of Reading. He gave the sum of £7,500 to be used for the purchase of a plot of land within the town to build a strong house with a garden fit for the poor to work in. The main trade to be carried out there would be cloth manufacture, dyeing and things allied to it.

According to his will, premises were purchased in Minster Street in 1625 and for many years it was a prosperous trade in the town, with the waterways so near, namely the River Kennet and the Thames.

Unfortunately, by 1812 the entire building was falling into a sad state of disrepair and ruin. During these years some of these premises were rented out for floor cloth manufacturing and sail machinery. In 1850, after many squabbles by the charities' commissioners and the beneficiaries of Christ's Hospital, The Oracle and its effects were sold and it later became a workhouse for the town.

Now in 1995 plans have been passed for the site to become one of the largest shopping areas in the south, to be known as The Oracle once again.

In 1789, James Cocks started the Reading sauce industry and in 1814 he registered his proprietary rights to his products in the law courts. This trade soon became known all over the country and abroad and business flourished right up until the late 1960s.

Of course, Reading became mostly known throughout the world for its other three main industries – beer, biscuits and bulbs

There were five breweries in Reading. The main one, Messrs Stephens, was said to produce 25,000 barrels of beer annually. Then in 1785, William Blackall Simonds established the firm of Simonds Brewery which was to become one of the largest in the world. It was established in Broad Street where it eventually covered many acres of land.

During the 18th and 19th centuries Reading had a thriving tanning industry and also brick works were established at Tilehurst where the clay was perfect for the manufacture of bricks. These brick fields occupied many acres and the clay was passed overhead in large buckets across busy roads to the kilns at Norcot where it was made into bricks. The sites of the kilns have now become housing estates.

Many people throughout the country and, indeed, the world, have known the town of Reading for the fine seeds and bulbs which were grown by the firm of Suttons Seeds. As you entered Reading from the A4, the Old Bath Road, you were met by many acres of all kinds of flowers. This is now a very select industrial estate.

Just beyond Suttons Seeds' trial grounds was the large Reading power station supplying the town and surrounding villages with power. This has now ceased and been pulled down.

In 1841, George Palmer came to Reading

and joined Thomas Huntley as a partner. They started the world famous Huntley & Palmer biscuit firm in a small shop at 72 London Street and by 1850 the firm was employing 200 people. I have devoted a whole section to Huntley & Palmers in the book.

We also look at some of the history of surrounding villages such as Goring-on-Thames with its old mill mentioned in Domesday Book, and Pangbourne, the home of the author Kenneth Graham who wrote *The Wind in the Willows*.

There is also the military village of Arborfield. Indeed, within an area of ten miles surrounding the historic town of Reading, in the heart of the Thames Valley, we have some of the most beautiful scenery in England.

Reading has always been a town which has expressed itself in the charm of its buildings. Unfortunately, for the last 50 years much of that charm and interest has been destroyed by the planners, and ugly office blocks put up all over the place.

However, the mistake has now been recognised by the authorities and much effort is being made to bring the beauty of Reading back with its old-world charm. I hope this book helps the reader recall those days.

Harold Hill
Reading
August 1995

Around the Town

One of the main arteries in and out of the town is the Oxford Road. The first part of it was, for most of this century, dominated by the largest department store in town, that of William McIlroy's, often called the Glass City or Reading Crystal Palace because, as you can see, it had some 23 enormous plate-glass windows and the building covered three streets, Oxford Street (later to be called Oxford Road), part of West Street and part of Cheapside, a street so called because in bygone days most small shops there sold things cheaply. Opposite McIlroy's were many well-known local firms such as Langston's the outfitters, Watts' the cycle shop, Edgar's the hairdressers and many more which, in the first 60 years of this century, were household names.

As this photograph, taken in 1910, well illustrates, further down Oxford Road there was a whole mass of small shops, the main one being Callas Sons & May Ltd. The picture also gives a clear view of the tramway system into Reading. Here also was a firm known as Jackson's Scrap Iron Works. In their yards one could find almost anything one wanted except, of course, car spares because the firm had not been in existence long enough to find themselves a breaker's yard.

We are now about three quarters of a mile outside the town centre, travelling along the Oxford Road and about to go under one of the most well-known railway bridges in Reading, called Reading West Bridge, over which trains pass continually to and from the West Country. The large advertisement for Newbury's Furniture was displayed on either side of this bridge for over half a century, as they were the leading furniture store in Reading.

One can clearly see the old original brick-built bridge at Reading West Bridge flooded during a heavy rain storm. Due to the dip in the roads to allow the trams to go under, and bad drainage, this happened every time there was torrential rain, hence the notice 'Keep your Seats'.

Here is the same section of the Oxford Road, this time showing one of the first horse-drawn trams in the town, *c*.1900. The illustration is from an original picture by Berkshire Books and Prints.

Leaving Reading on the Oxford Road, one sees the large building of Brock Barracks, built by Major Flint of the Royal Engineers in 1877. For most of this century the Barracks has been the home of the Royal Berkshire Regiment, although during World War Two there were many regiments from all over the world stationed there including those from the United States and Canada. The various regiments often caused great interest as they marched the two miles from the Barracks to the Railway Station, led by their appropriate military bands.

    In 1959 the Barracks ceased to be the home of the Royal Berkshires, upon their amalgamation with the Wiltshire Regiment which ultimately formed the Duke of Edinburgh's Royal Regiment. The Barracks has also been rather proud of its Museum of Militaria. Sadly, whilst the building still stands and small parts are used for minor military purposes, most of it has become a housing estate.

Just a few hundred yards down the road from Brock Barracks we come to the old Pond House pub. During the days of the trams this became a well-known name in Reading as it was the terminus and in the early part of this century many people would board a tram in Broad Street and journey down the three miles of Oxford Road to the Pond House terminus just for the thrill of the ride.

A little journey back towards Reading takes us into Broad Street, but before we get there we must pass the many small shops which make up these three miles of Oxford Road which has changed little over the last 75 years. On the left is the West Reading Methodist Church which dates back over 100 years.

Oxford Road from the crossroads of West Street.

Part of Oxford Road, Reading, by Western Elms Avenue and Beresford Road.

Further down the Oxford Road stands the old Battle Hospital which started its life as a workhouse for the poor people of the town.

Nearly in the same section of Oxford Road is the Reading West Bridge.

Broad Street, the widest and most important street in Reading, holds many memories for thousands of local people over this century. The section pictured here at the end of the last century is an area that has seen vast changes over the last 50 years. The area on the left, from what used to be the Waterloo House Hotel and almost to the entrance to the arcade *(see page 15, top)*, is now taken over mostly by the Marks & Spencer department store. On the left just before the hotel from the 1930s to the 1960s was Walter C.Hunt's corn and seed merchants, and the Maypole Grocery Store, Kendalls umbrellas and the Bull Hotel on the corner of Cross Street.

Here, as we continue down Broad Street, we see a typical example of the amount of small shops in this street, for the picture is dominated by the arcade entrance leading to the Corn Exchange. The sign of the Victoria Café, a leading restaurant, stands out. On this side of the arcade was Walker Stores, one of the main grocer's in the town. Opposite the statue of George Palmer (one of the founders of Huntley and Palmers Biscuits) is the well-known firm of Butler's menswear, still in existence today in Broad Street.

The arcade shown in the previous photograph on page 14, leading to the Corn Exchange, is a good example of Reading's small businesses in the first quarter of this century. Note the Edwardian style gas lights over each stall. Many businesses were started here and went on to become larger shops in the town. Also note the newsagent's on the left, typical of a time when the main way to advertise was to plaster the place with posters.

We cross the road in Broad Street to one of the street's main department stores, Wellsteed's, all dressed up for King George V's coronation in 1911. In the centre of the road can be seen two young boys who would wait there to be called to the office in the arcade opposite, from where they would be dispatched to deliver a parcel or letter locally around the area. This service was run by Reading Corporation Transport.

Just further down from Wellsteed's up until 1904 was the Speedwell Motor Company, in the building which was once Walsingham House, the home of Lord Walsingham. The Speedwell Motor Company was established to assemble, amongst other models, the French Dedion cars, an example of which can be seen in this picture outside their showroom. The author's grandfather had such a car which he remembers riding in as a child. The very last car to be assembled at this works in 1904 was the Dedion Dogcart, still being used today by an executive of the *Evening Post* in the London-Brighton car rally.

The traffic had increased considerably when this picture was taken in the early 1930s. On the left is the large department store of Heelas, then privately owned but today belonging to the John Lewis Partnership. The main street lighting was still from those grand old gas lights, and there were no controlled crossings – pedestrians just hoped they could make it in between the cars and trams.

Opposite the Heelas store is the third large department store of A.H.Bull, seen in the distance behind the second tram. Another well-known firm is E.Hill & Sons, who were famed for their high-class fancy goods and baby carriages. Most of these shops have now been taken over and turned into the large store of W.H.Smith Ltd.

On the left-hand side further up from Heelas is the narrow lane of Chain Street, so called because it runs from Broad Street to Gun Street and often became so congested with small hand carts making a short cut for deliveries that it was chained off by the Corporation at busy times.

On the corner of Broad Street at the end of the last century stood the old White Hart Hotel. In a sad state of repair even then, it was eventually demolished.

The main place of worship in Broad Street was the Broad Street Chapel, seen here in the background from Chesterman's fruit shop. It is only in the last three years that it has ceased as a chapel and is now to become a large bookshop.

Broad Street in the 1950s with the then modern façade of F.W.Woolworth on the left. In the distance can be seen the large clock of H.Samuel's the Jeweller.

Looking down Oxford Street, on the left is the old Vine public house, looking down towards A.H.Bull & co, whose blinds are out.

In the early part of this century, this ancient street had many old buildings still very much in use, but as you will see, most of them have now been demolished and replaced. Here is Friar Street looking towards the Town Hall in 1882.

Until just before World War Two, one of the main buildings in Friar Street was the Royal County Theatre which is pictured here on the right. It was well known for its musical shows and Christmas pantomimes. Alas, it was burned down in 1937 during a pantomime season. There were no casualties but this grand theatre was completely destroyed, never to be rebuilt.

This photograph shows Friar Street in the 1950s with the Central Cinema on the right. Next to it stood two well-known firms of Fidler's seeds and Viden's florist, and beside them the high-class jewellers of Winches'. On the first floor of the Central Cinema was a dancing school where you could learn how to foxtrot or waltz around the ballroom to the sound of Victor Sylvester.

Turning into Friar Street from Station Road, you are faced with a whole selection of different Victorian and Edwardian buildings. The old established music store of Hickie and Hickie, clearly seen in this picture, is still in business today.

It is said that when Queen Victoria visited Reading she was disgusted with her reception, and so when George Blackwell Simonds made the statue of her which was erected in 1857, she insisted that it stood with its back to the town. This area, as you can see, was also the main rank for hansom cabs.

The Victorian architecture of Reading Town Hall, which was started in 1875 but not completed until 1882, is still one of the finest buildings in the town. On the left used to stand the Queen's Hotel and the General Post Office. Also pictured is the ancient church of St Lawrence's, founded in 1121 and which has always played a leading part in ceremonial occasions in Reading. The author has often sat quietly here, looking at the stained glass window, his imagination drifting back 1,000 years, to a time when the church was part of the abbey.

Until the early 1950s, Friar Street was always dominated by the Blagrave Buildings, a block of Victorian flats, seen here on the left.

The attractive village of Caversham, now almost a main part of Reading and yet keeping its own identity, can be entered only by going over one or the other bridges. On the original thirteenth-century wooden bridge the Royalist defenders of Caversham were defeated by the Roundheads, and on the island between the bridges Robert de Montford fought a duel with Henry de Essex whilst watched by Henry II. This illustration shows the iron bridge, built in the first part of this century, with St Peter's Church in the background.

Caversham is a giant mix of houses of all shapes and sizes as the village grew and many dwellings were added. What sure makes it such an interesting place is the varied selection of architecture, as can be seen here in Bridge Street.

Of course, the dominating feature about Caversham is the charm of the river frontage stretching right along the banks of the village with the wide expanse of water suitable for all forms of boating and steamer trips.

In the previous picture you caught a glimpse of a wooden framework in the right-hand channel of the river. Here you have a clearer view of what were the eel traps which were lowered at night and brought up in the morning when the eels were removed. Some were sold to the pie and eel shop which stood by the bridge until the 1920s. A pie and eel breakfast was purchased by men going into Reading to work.

The charming church of St Peter's, which dates from Saxon times, stands proud on the hill overlooking the river.

The main attraction in Reading is always the river which is more popular today but spoilt by the many motor launches which queue up all day through the summer to use the lock pictured here. In the background is the famous Clappers, built to control the fast flow of water over this wide expanse of the Thames. You can walk right across these and come out at the lock, but it can be quite terrifying as you see thousands of gallons of water going over the weirs beneath your feet.

Up until World War Two there were some fine old boathouses by the Thames at Caversham and on weekends local people would queue up to hire out boats for the day, whether it was a skiff, a punt or a rowing boat. When this photograph was taken there were not many motor boats or launches about.

Caversham is made up of small, fairly narrow streets such as Church Street, which was always a pleasure to walk along in bygone days when the road was fairly free from traffic, just the occasional horse and cart or pony and trap. The paths were so narrow that pedestrians had to step into the road to pass someone with a perambulator, which in those days were quite large.

The other main street in Caversham is Prospect Street, which as you can see, although it is a main artery of the village, was very quiet when this picture was taken in 1910.

As you go out of Caversham towards Woodcote and Wallingford, you have to go up St Peter's Hill, the entrance to the church of that name is seen on the left.

Further up the hill you have one of the old parts of the village known as The Warren, seen here.

This long and very charming journey down The Warren has many beautiful houses.

At the entrance to The Warren stands this old thatched cottage as it was at the turn of the century.

As you travel further down The Warren you go out into the country and yet you are less than a mile from Caversham village.

Here is the main shopping street of Prospect Street, Caversham, as it was *c*.1910.

Caversham has had its fair share of floods as illustrated in this view in 1947.

Another view of the floods in Caversham.

Here you see a west view of the old Caversham Bridge when it was a part-brick and part-wooden construction.

This view of Caversham Bridge from St Peter's Hill is a fine example of the expanse of land which was there in the seventeenth century.

Here you see a fine view of the bridge and the cottage that was moved 25ft for the construction of the iron bridge.

Another view of the iron bridge which replaced the brick and wooden bridge which was in use until the present concrete one was opened in 1926.

One of the main attractions of Caversham has always been the wide expanse of the Thames as pictured here.

Beside the Thames at Caversham there was, until the 1970s, the beautiful old Caversham Bridge Hotel.

Just down the road as we leave the bridge we find Bridge Street with its mixture of houses and the old Crown pub.

Hemdean Road-Grove Hill junction with the aged protected tree, a landmark for many years.

Before the onset of the motor launch, this view of the lock from a rowing boat or punt was always a delight to behold.

On the left as you enter the lock is a large weir known locally as The Clappers, where, it is said, in the early part of this century a certain lady who was a nanny threw a child or children over the weir and drowned them.

Caversham Church Street as it was at the turn of the century.

The old White Hart Inn which stood at the entrance to the old Caversham Bridge. This picture was taken before 1869.

As you will see from this photograph, rowing was not the only popular pastime before World War Two. Freebody's Lido attracted hundreds of people on sunny days.

Caversham Lock as it was in 1912. In those days a popular thing to do was to walk by the river and end up at the lock to watch the boats go through.

This view of Caversham Lock from a different angle shows the well-known pre-war boat house of John Tims & Sons.

Another attraction beside the Thameside promenade was the paddling pool for the very young children.

Whitley Pump, which used to stand at the top of this street, was well known to stagecoach drivers and local tradesman with their horse and carts, as the stop where they could water their horses. History records that in about 1810 a man who was starving and who had a wife and four young children, was caught in the act of stealing a loaf of bread. He was chased up Silver Street, which leads into Whitley Street, and was hanged, without trial, from a tree.

Caversham Bridge Hotel overshadows the boats and boathouse. The location has changed out of all recognition compared with this picture.

Another, much clearer view of the old Whitley Pump as it was in 1921 with a police officer from Reading Borough Police posing for the picture. It is understood that he was off duty at the time.

Just a few hundred yards east from the pump is another famous road with one of Reading's most well-known schools, that of Abbey School in Kendrick Road.

Whitley Street pump, famous over the centuries as a drinking trough for tradesmen's horses.

The once tiny village of Tilehurst is situated on the outskirts of Reading, although it is not so tiny today but vastly over populated. This picture shows one of the lanes which used to be called Chapel Hill, where there used to stand a small galvanised tin hut used as a chapel. Rumour has it that one day a man was praying in the chapel when he was murdered. His killer was hanged at Oxford Prison.

Just down the road from Chapel Hill used to be another charming lane, called Church Road, shown here at the turn of the century with hardly a house in sight. Today it is a built-up area.

This view looks down on Tilehurst from Arthur Newbury Park. Mr Newbury was a well-respected businessman in the town for nearly 50 years, hence the park being named after him. The wide expanse of open ground and trees has long since gone, to be replaced all around by hundreds of houses.

Many of the roads in the village of Tilehurst were tree-lined, such as Park Lane, shown here with a trolley bus in the distance heading into town.

Many of the houses built in the Victorian and Edwardian eras still lend quiet peace and charm to the old village of Tilehurst, such as Armour Road, shown here in 1910 with the old gas lights and with local people walking in peace.

Just down the road in Tilehurst can be found the beautiful River Thames. On its bank stands the large hotel once called the Roebuck, now called Beethoven's. It was from this hotel, which stands on the main Reading-Oxford road, that the Berkshire Hunt used to set out, often with King Edward VII or other royalty, to hunt foxes across the open fields of Tilehurst and the adjoining village of Purley.

During World War One, in a field opposite this inn, were between 600 and 1,000 horses which were trained there before going on active service. It was known as a Remount Depot under the command of Captain Cecil Aldin. He was a personal friend of King Edward VII and they often hunted together. Readers may recall the name of Cecil Aldin as one of the most famous artists of the late nineteenth and early twentieth century, much admired for his series of old coaching inns of England and his brilliant drawings and paintings of dogs.

Along the Thames used to be a lido, used extensively until the start of World War Two. This picture shows the ladies' swimming race at Tilehurst Regatta around 1910.

Westwood Road, Tilehurst, is an area which mostly grew in Edwardian and Victorian times with an assortment of varying designed houses.

St Michael's Road, Tilehurst, is one of the more modern roads with most of the houses pictured here built in the 1930s.

School Road, Tilehurst, is today one of the busiest parts of the village, but when this picture was taken about 1920 it had little traffic to disturb the tranquillity of the place.

In the first part of this century the village of Tilehurst did not consist of many roads compared with today, although it was one of the largest parishes in Reading, stretching right out to Theale. This is another quiet road of the village, Blundells Road.

There are three roads in the Armour category, Armour Road, this one Lower Armour Road and Armour Hill. Each road had its own character in the old village.

St Michael's Parish Church has always had considerable influence in the area.

In the 1940s, Tilehurst really came alive with improvements to the roads and with the introduction of the trolley buses it was a good opportunity for Reading Borough Council to improve the area. This is the Triangle at Tilehurst.

The White House pub has been a landmark in Tilehurst for most of this century. This part of the village has altered little over the years.

With the introduction of the trolley buses, of course, termini had to be built. This is Church Road terminus at Tilehurst.

One of the largest housing developments in Tilehurst has been the Berkshire Drive area. This picture shows the beginnings of the estate some 30 years ago.

One of the main arteries leading from Reading's Oxford Road to Tilehurst is Norcot Road. This photograph shows part of the junction to School Road from Norcot Hill.

Built in the first part of this century, the Tilehurst water tower stands proud and high as a landmark to all of those entering the village.

In Victorian and Edwardian times the upper portion of King's Road, one of the main arteries of Reading, was mainly a line of élite houses, many built of Bath Stone. They still stand very elegantly, although most of them have been restored. In the middle of King's Road was a square of similar houses known as Victoria Square, the pillars of which are just visible at the entrance to this rather exclusive square. Here, in this picture of *c.*1890, can be seen horse-drawn trams on their journey from Brock Barracks in the Oxford Road to Palmer Park.

Proceeding further up King's Road we enter the era of the electric trams which replaced that of the old horse-drawn ones. The old gas lamps and the charm of the standards in the centre of the road were a beauty to behold, although it was probably taken for granted in those days.

At the Cemetery Junction, where King's Road, London Road and Wokingham Road meet, used to stand the monumental works of McCarthy E.Fitt, pictured here at the turn of the century.

In this section on King's Road, leading to the Cemetery Junction, we can clearly see on the left the horse trough used, until 1920, by tradesmen to water their horses.

As we go out of Reading from either King's Road or London Road, we have to converge with the Cemetery Junction. During the last century this became a very busy place and as you can see many shops sprang up including this large Co-operative shop, built in 1900.

St Bartholemew's Church on the main A4 Long Road, Reading, as it was in 1905.

This picture, taken in 1955, shows the Cemetery Junction with the trolley bus wires overhead and the old tramlines still there. In the centre is a police officer on duty in his box, controlling one set of traffic lights. On the left is the Marquis of Granby public house which was used by stagecoach drivers as a stop-over before they went into the town or on their way to Bristol and Oxford.

Travelling along Wokingham Road from the cemetery we come to Palmer Park, situated between London Road (the A4) and Wokingham Road. The park has brought pleasure to tens of thousands of people over the last 100 years.

One of the major activities in Palmer Park has been the ancient game of bowls. Here is one of the bowling greens in the park with the pavilion in the background.

As can be seen from this picture, in the first part of this century Palmer Park was a main gathering point for sports and social events. Note the penny-farthing bicycles of the men gathered outside the park gates when this picture was taken *c.*1890. The park still holds its beauty to a certain extent today, although many more buildings have been built upon it. There is a fine running track, a large library and an excellent children's playground. The sports facilities are floodlit to enable evening events but this has meant that the park itself has lost a lot of its 'old world' charm.

The fine Victorian gates that enhanced the entrance to Palmer Park.

Until it was moved to Palmer Park when the tram lines were taken up, the statue of George Palmer dominated Broad Street for half a century.

Although the trams rattled by, all was silent inside the Royal Berkshire Hospital as the nurses attended the sick.

One of the town's finest buildings, Royal Berkshire Hospital was opened in 1830. There are too many to count who owe their lives to the skill and dedication of the doctors and nurses at this still very fine institution.

Once it was pleasant to stroll along London Road which was then tree-lined. Notice the open lawns in the front, now a car park.

London Street, one of the oldest streets in Reading, with its cobbled stone street which was taken up in the 1950s.

Another grand old pub which has always been a landmark as you enter Reading from the London Road is the Marquis of Granby, pictured here *c.*1900.

A view of the Forbury Gardens.

Queen Elizabeth II and the Duke of Edinburgh visit Reading for the opening of the new university in 1953.

The Maiwand Lion, erected in Forbury Gardens in 1886 in honour of the men of the Royal Berkshire Regiment who gave their lives at the Battle of Maiwand in the Afghan War of 1879-80.

In the centre of Forbury Gardens has always stood the fountain and fish pond, now sadly fallen into disrepair.

A few yards from the Maiwand Lion is the bandstand where local and military bands have entertained members of the public for years.

The ancient ruins of the Abbey still stand proud and as a tourist attraction.

A little further along from the Abbey Gateway used to stand the headquarters of Berkshire County Police, since demolished to make way for new Law Courts.

This engraving gives us an insight to the old Abbey Gateway.

Queen Victoria Street as it was in the 1920s when it was one of the most exclusive shopping streets in Reading.

A more up-to-date picture of Jackson's Corner in the 1950s.

It was a busy day when this picture was taken at Jackson's Corner.

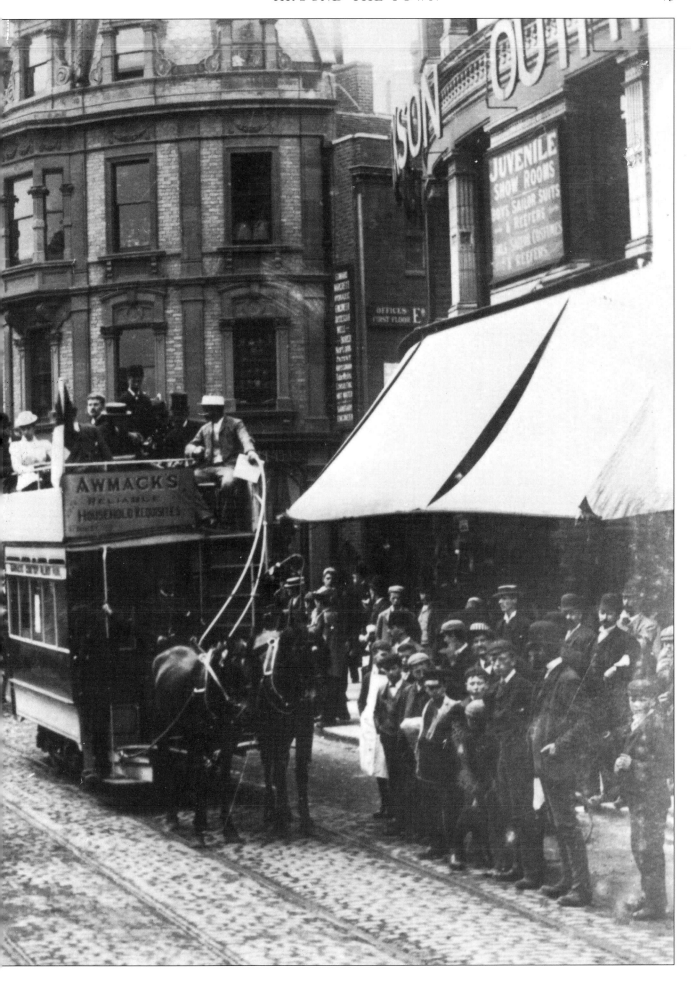

This is old Duke Street as it was at the turn of the century, a thriving little centre of small shops now mostly gone.

Another plate from *Manns History of Reading*, an east view of High Bridge in Bridge Street (Duke Street).

King's Street, Reading, has always been one of the busy thoroughfares of the town as this picture of the nineteenth century shows.

For centuries the Butter Market had been a busy small market on Saturdays. Alas, it is no longer used for this purpose.

Another view of the Butter Market with St Lawrence's Church dominating the skyline.

On Saturday the crowds would gather in the Butter Market when traders would come in with their wares, such as you see here with Wilder's who sold farm implements.

Another view of the Market Place on a weekday with their many small shops which so attracted people.

In the 1950s the main market was still held in the old Butter Market.

Ancient Cross Street dating back to the thirteenth century and originally known as Gutter Lane, seen here in 1887.

Reading Jail when it was Greyfriars Church in the middle of the last century.

In the 1920s many of roads in the Reading area were resurfaced and one of the main streets to come under reconstruction was Friar Street.

Up a little further is West Street was Fortescues, where you could buy almost anything.

Up Union Street ('Smelly Alley') from Broad Street to Friar Street, just around the corner was the well-known small café of S.C.Leaity with its personal and homely service.

Each Boxing Day the hunters and the foxhounds would gather outside the Town Hall to be sent on one of their hunts by a large crowd of local well wishers.

One of the best known local grocers in Reading and Caversham was Bayliss & Co.

High Bridge towards the town and Jackson's Corner *c.*1910.

Looking the other way down High Bridge, now often called Duke Street Bridge, with the old Reading Borough Police Station centre left. This was later used as a Coroner's Court and is now solicitors' offices.

One of Reading's charming old inns on the way out to Wokingham is the George and Dragon beside the River Kennett.

Another engraving which caused quite a lot of controversy when it was published in *Manns History of Reading* showed a south view of the supposed ruins of the castle.

Market Place in Reading as it was in 1823.

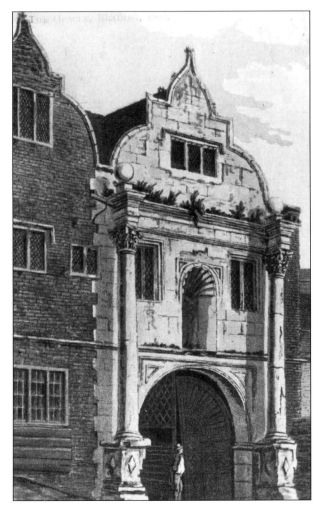

A drawing of the old
Oracle Gateway which
was built by John Kendrick
as a cotton mill and later
became Reading's largest
workhouse.

Long since gone are the railings that used to surround the churchyard. This picture *c.*1920 shows the tram wire and rails.

St Mary's Butts when the motor car and motor bus had taken over from the horse and cart.

Looking up St Mary's Butts in the 1950s.

The largest pre-war department store in the town was McIlroy's which stretched into three streets and was known as Reading's 'Crystal Palace' because of its mass of plate-glass windows. It employed about 300 people and had its own chapel for the many staff who lived in.

St Mary's Butts in the late 1920s. Note the solid tyres on the old omnibus. Even in those days there were such things as rifle ranges and the well-known local milliners, Calvert & Tilley.

Two shops dominated this section of St Mary's Butts on the corner of Hosier Street. They were Herbert & Lascelles electrical shop, and Pickfords removals firm.

On the opposite side of the town is Coley Avenue, pictured in the 1930s. It led down to Coley House, the home of the Vachell family and where Charles I once stayed.

Back to Castle Street, to the old coaching stables, which were mostly underground in the last century.

Castle Street, Reading, with the factory of Ferguson's Ales and Stouts on the left centre.

A tram wends its way up Castle Street to Bath Road *c.*1920.

Further down Castle Street is St Mary's Church. On the left, the old Higgs Brewery stood next to the Sun public house.

Part of Castle Street from the turnpike entering Reading.

The two railway bridges which overpower all the beauty of the river at Newtown, *c.*1930.

The almost deserted old Bath Road at Reading at the turn of the century.

This is the fine Reading Bridge, opened in 1923 with its large single arch.

Just a few hundred yards from the Royal Berkshire Hospital stands the more modern buildings of Reading University.

The spire of St Giles' Church has been a landmark for miles around as it dominates Southampton Street.

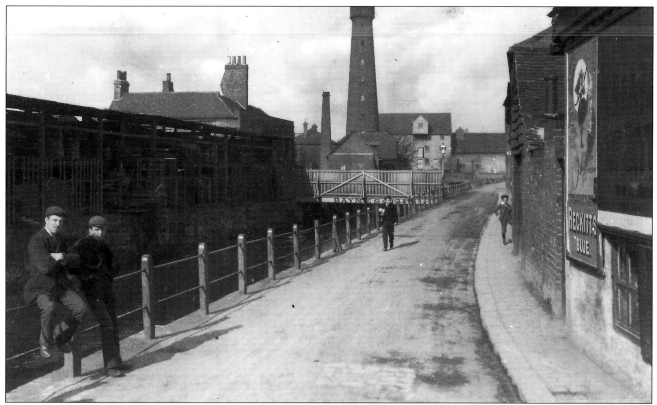

Mill Lane, so called because of the large St Giles Mill which dominated it.

For nearly a century, Reading was hit by floods, as here *c.*1894.

This part of Reading is now unrecognisable compared to when John Lines on the corner of Blagrave Street in sight of the Town Hall stood here *c.*1950.

The Little Crown public house, Southampton Street, in the 1950s.

Brook Street, Coley, with the River Kennett flowing past beyond the railings. The flags are out for the Coronation of Queen Elizabeth II.

The widest part of Broad Street in the 1950s, with Marks & Spencer on the left.

At the bottom of London Street stood two large buildings; one was Hugh Wyllie's, the credit drapers, and the other (just seen extreme right) was Bradley & Bliss, the town's wholesale chemist.

Southampton Street just before St Giles's Church. The scene has changed little over the years.

Until the 1960s, there were rows of small traders where the Inner Distribution Road now stands.

On this site now stands the Broad Street Mall and the Ramada Hotel; this is how it was until the early 1960s.

The building of Chatham Street car park.

This is Southcote Manor which was, in Elizabethan times, the home of John Blagrave and his family, one of the most brilliant mathematicians of his time. In the Civil War, Cromwell held council here with Essex and and Blake. There are still traces of the 30ft-wide moat around the houses which now stand on the site.

The estate of Southcote has arisen since the last war but the history of this place goes back for centuries. Most of the fields here were farm land for over 700 years. Here you see the gatehouse in 1921, in a sad state of disrepair.

Across the road from Southcote is the beautiful Prospect Park, one of the finest open areas in the town. It was originally 120 acres of timber land and on it stands this beautiful seventeenth-century mansion house. It was handed over to Reading Borough Council in 1911 on the condition that its present acreage was not reduced or sold off; by that time the 120 acres had been reduced to its present 12 acres.

Mr Salmet used to give flights in his hand-made aeroplane from the meadows by the river.

Industry and Commerce

In the first half of this century there was one large commercial vehicle firm, the Great Western Motors seen here *c.*1920.

The Royal Visit to SUTTON'S at READING.

IN THE VEGETABLE SEED ORDER ROOM

BIRD'S-EYE VIEW OF THE ROYAL SEED ESTABLISHMENT

The Royal Visit to SUTTON'S at READING.

Beside Huntley & Palmer's, one of the largest firms in Reading was that of Sutton's Seeds whose head office was in the Market Place. Here, King Edward VII visited the factory.

Heelas department store started in a very small way over 100 years ago.

Trolley buses were the main means of transport up until the 1960s – fast, no fumes and reliable.

This is the delivery lorry of the South Berks Brewery, one of the many smaller brewers in the area *c.*1930.

Before World War Two, there were two main coal merchants in Reading – C.& G.Ayres and, shown in this picture, G.W.Talbot & Sons.

This is one of the old steam-driven delivery lorries of H.&.G.Simonds the brewers.

Another steam-driven lorry, used for the delivery of grain from James Dewe's Burghfield Mills.

Do you remember the days when the first pint of milk came from the large churn into your jug? This is the well-known local milkman of Williams & Son, Oxford Road, Reading.

Right up until the late 1960s one could often see herds of cattle being driven up Caversham Road to the Cattle Market just around the corner in Great Knolly's Street.

If you wanted your fortune told, you would go to the Romany gypsy at her caravan in Newtown.

Another flourishing trade in the town before the onset of canned drinks were the minerals delivered to the door by the local firm of Tunbridge Jones & Co.

Another view of the old Heelas delivery vans, used for furniture removals.

Many small industries flourished well up until the 1960s. This is Marsh & Co at their iron and engineering works at Short Street.

The small grocer was in much demand before supermarkets. One of these was Coles, of Oxford Road.

Many small pubs in Reading were so cosy in the old days. One such pub is the Plough Inn at Tilehurst, pictured as it was here in the 1930s. It retains its old-world charm today.

Roadside trades also flourished, such as this man who used to sit at the bottom of Grovelands Road mending chairs.

One well-known shop was that run by Henry Coxhead and his wife in Union Street, locally known as Smelly Alley due to the many fish and meat shops there.

Another unusual shop in Union Street was that of W.H.Moore, the specialist knife oulet.

The old Vaudeville Cinema as it was in Broad Street in the 1920s.

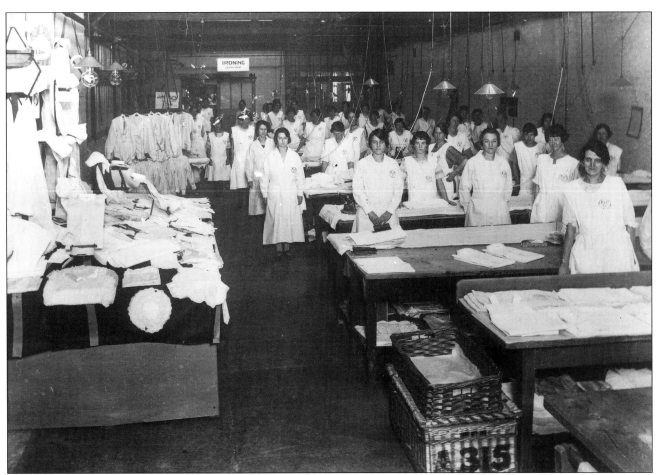

This is Reading and Caversham laundry *c.*1920s.

One of the many young ladies who helped the war effort at a factory near Reading.

The ladies of Reading could be seen working in fields in the Land Army.

Romany caravans, manufactured with pride by Vincent's of Reading.

This was one of the Ilsley's Tilehurst buses, started in 1900 to take people from Tilehurst into town and at the same time advertising the department store of A.H.Bull Ltd.

More up to date in the 1960s was a well-known firm of Brennan's which stood at the bottom of London Street and made its name selling army surplus.

The old seed firm of Sutton's Seeds was known throughout the world. This was one of their main buildings with its Victorian façade. The main shop was in the Market Place and the trial grounds were on the main London Road at Earley.

The Market Place was dominated by the old-established firm of Hill's Rubber Company.

In Victorian and Edwardian times many schools were built in Reading, in particular in East Reading due to the growth of the population in that area with the expansion of Huntley and Palmer's. This is Alfred Sutton's School, on the right in Wokingham Road. It is still a school today.

Over this last century, Reading Corporation Transport has always employed a fine body of men and women and there has seldom been a dispute with this well-run service. This is the RCT Home Guard during World War Two.

Reading Corporation Transport had their own football team. Here are some of the players in the 1930s.

Members of the Reading Corporation Transport in the 1920s.

Not only did the Reading Corporation Transport workers play football, but they also did a lot of charity work. Here they are throwing a Christmas party for local children.

In 1841, George Palmer came to Reading and went into partnership with Thomas Huntley and started Huntley & Palmer's at 72 London Street, Reading, in 1850. By 1857, 200 people worked there and a few years later they were employing 1,300.

Huntley & Palmer's factory in King's Road in the 1860s.

At the turn of the century, Huntley & Palmer's were the biggest employers in the town.

The girls' packing room (north) at the King's Road factory at the end of the nineteenth century.

The spirit amongst the workers at Huntley & Palmer's was always good and this is typical of one of the parties which took place in their social club.

The Huntley & Palmer's factory in more modern times.

The production line in the 1950s, where the popular water biscuits were produced at thousands per hour.

Above: One of Huntley & Palmer's delivery vans.

Below: The *Queen of the Thames* was owned by Maynard's steamers and brought a lot of pleasure to thousands of people on their river trips.

The full extent of the Huntley & Palmer's factory at its height in the 1950s.

Reading even had its own factory for tobacco until a few years ago with the old established firm of Brigham & Sons at 94 London Street, Reading.

Blundell's was a good family firm of grocers in the Oxford Road on the corner of Gower Street, in the days when the fashion was to cover the walls and windows with advertising posters.

There were many small bakeries in the town and one of the leading ones was the family firm of Tibble's Bakery. Note the small delivery carts waiting to be harnessed to their horses.

In Castle Street was the old established firm of Lion Brewery, owned by the family of S.H.Higgs.

Wet or fine, you would find the coal being delivered by Mr W.Brown down the Oxford Road – hard work from a well-respected man.

One of the largest delivery and storage firms in Reading up until the 1970s was that of Ayres Ltd. They were also the largest coal merchants in the area.

The family firm of Heelas expanded their department store in Broad Street to have one of the largest depositories in the town. They were also one of the largest house furnishers as well and the much expanded firm still trades today, although now owned by the John Lewis group.

This is how one of the town's largest grocers in the 1950s started at the turn of the century, going on after the last war to run a fleet of mobile grocery shops.

Once the motor car became established in Reading, many garages sprung up to sell them to the public. One of the best known was the Royal Berks Motor Company, founded by Mr Ted Thomas. This photograph shows the garage in Thorn Street in 1927.

Typical of one of the dozens of small shops there were all over Reading in the first part of this century, this family grocers was in the covered arcade in Broad Street.

People and Places

A trip back in time to a county school as it was in the first quarter of this century. These were the pupils of Theale School with their teacher.

Rowing is one of the most popular sports in Reading. Here in the 1950s, the Reading Iris Rowing Club sets out on a practice at the Dreadnought.

Members of the Reading Iris Rowing Club having just received their new trophy.

One way to get to know your neighbour was to join forces and go on a steamer outing as this group did in the 1930s.

There has always been a strong contingent of the Boys' Brigade in Reading and it is still going strong today.

One very enchanting public house until it was rebuilt early this century was the Griffin at Caversham, pictured here as it was in 1890.

Another ancient coaching inn, known as The Broadface in The High in Reading, has long since gone.

A few hundred yards from The Broadface is The Upper Ship in Duke Street with its centuries of history.

As you travelled out of Reading to journey to Wokingham or Earley you came to the Three Tuns, one of Simond's early public houses.

Or if you travelled to Burghfield, you could call in to the Rising Sun.

If you go along the main A4 and head for the charming village of Beenham you will find a pub with the unusual name of The Stocks.

Staying in the country areas we find another old public house as it was nearly a hundred years ago at Brimpton.

Bringing our short journey of old pubs up to the 1960s is one very popular public house in the town centre of Reading, The Jolly Porter, so named because it was opposite the main railway station.

Law and Order

The Reading Police centenary parade at Police College, Sulhampstead, in 1956 led by an Austin A95.

In 1966, Reading Borough Police took delivery of Norton 750cc motorcycles, seen here in Oxford Road.

A proud officer stands beside his new Berkshire Constabulary Austin 110 Westminster in 1966.

PC Ray Hunt on the new Triumph Speed Twin outside the old County Police HQ in Abbey Square (now demolished) in 1949.

Into the Countryside

In the first part of this century, all around the countryside of Reading there were old country trades. Here is a milk maid.

On Sunday afternoons, the Lady of the Manor would take her children out for a ride in the donkey and trap.

Country children had to amuse themselves with hand-made toys, such as the hoop and the wooden wheel barrow.

In the summer months, many a Sunday afternoon was taken up with hay making in the fields.

Dad would go for his pint at the local in his donkey and cart.

In 1891, Berkshire had one of its hardest winters for years which even froze the River Thames. These two men are standing on the frozen lock at Sonning.

This was followed by one of the worst blizzards in memory, as the above picture of Sonning shows, but of course since then we have endured similar severe winters, in 1947 and 1963.

This is how delightful the lock at Sonning usually looked in the peace and tranquillity of its surroundings.

Just a few hundred yards up the road from the lock we come to the old-world setting and the village of Sonning. This is the High Street.

The old brick-built bridge at Sonning with the charming span of 11 arches can be seen from the bank of the Thames. In the background is the church with its fifteenth-century tower; indeed parts of of the church date back to the thirteenth and fourteenth centuries.

The view of the old cottages in the village of Sonning, some with Tudor-style fronts, are a delight to see.

This is a typical view as it was in Sonning village at the turn of the century.

One of the most picturesque communities in the surrounds of Reading is the beautiful village of Sonning.

Sonning, standing on the banks of the Thames with views which have been painted by artists from all over the world, is still as charming with its old buildings like the French Horn and the Old White Hart.

Down the Thames from Reading we have the still quiet village of Wargrave. The High Street has changed little, apart from the now constant flow of traffic.

Beyond the houses we have the peaceful waters of the Thames near Wargrave.

Wargrave once had a thriving business in the hiring out of skiffs, punts and rowing boats.

Down at Wargrave village the crowds gather around the shell of the burnt-out parish church, now beautifully restored. Rumour had it that it was burnt down by the Suffragette movement, but this has since been contradicted.

Around the surrounding villages of Reading used to stand many mills. One of the largest is Sindlesham Mill, near Earley, now a beautifully restored four-star restaurant and hotel complex.

The old Mapleduram Post Office, just a stone's throw from the famous mill.

This is the centuries old Mapleduram Mill, one of the few remaining mills still in use as a flour mill today.

Along the Three Mile Cross Road were many old pubs such as the George and Dragon.

In the Three Mile Cross area is the old pond, still there today and made famous by the author Mary Mitford who lived nearby at Swallowfield.

Back out on to the A4 London-Bath road, five miles outside of Reading, once stood one of the most famous coaching inns in the area The Angel Inn at Theale. On this site now stands the United Reform Church.

Twyford is about six miles from Reading just off the A4 to London and on the banks of the River Loddon. The Wagon and Horses is one of the old pubs in Twyford.

The bridge over the Loddon from the old London-Reading A4 coaching road, Twyford.

The Henley-Twyford road, pictured here as it was in the 1920s.

When Brunel bought the railway as far as Maidenhead and then on to Reading, he decided that Twyford was important enough to have a main line station.

London Road, Twyford, as it was in 1910 with a charm about it which has now gone.

On the other side of Reading, about four miles along the A4, is the village of Aldermaston, known now as the home of atomic energy. The charm of it as it is in this picture has long since gone.

On the banks of the Thames, about three miles from Goring, stands the old Beetle and Wedge Inn. It also used to be the ferry point taking you from the village of South Stoke to the main road at Streatley.

Another small village which has become a household name in many parts of the country is the garrison village of Arborfield, again mentioned by Mary Mitford, although she called it Arberliegh. It is also on the banks of the River Loddon.

Around the villages within a few miles from Reading is the ancient village of Bucklebury. It was here on the Common that Oliver Cromwell camped with 20,000 men. This was the old foundry at the turn of the century.

Further up the old Bath Road to London from Reading is Hare Hatch and the old pub, the Horse and Groom.

In the first part of this century, on what became the old B945 out of Reading, you would have come to the Alhambra Cottages in the village of Mortimer. This once quiet village is now a fast growing community of modern houses.

The old mill at Goring, pictured here *c.*1880, and, indeed, the village of Goring can be traced back to the Domesday Book.

The lock at Goring still holds as much charm today as it did when this picture was taken around 1930.

Just out of Goring is the small farming area of Gatehampton. This view is of the Thames, the Streatley Hills and the Brunel railway bridge, known locally as the Four Arches.

The two river bridges *c.*1910 with the old toll house which used to stand at the division of the Goring and Streatley Bridges.

The old bridge pictured from the Streatley side with the toll gates seen at the end of this section of the bridge.

One of the oldest hotels in the village of Goring is the Miller of Mansfield seen here on the left *c.*1920.

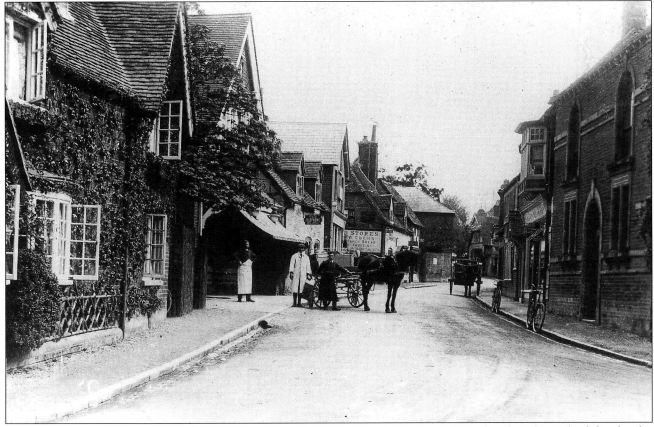

Goring has always had a good selection of shops in the High Street. On the right is the chapel; on the left – by the milk delivery horse and cart with the blinds out – is the local butcher's.

Along the banks of the River Thames there has always been a good selection for fishing.

Goring Lock with the church in the background with its Norman tower.

Here is a good view of the local parish church of St Thomas's, seen from the Thames backwater.

Every year until the first part of this century, the Goring Regatta was held. Here, crowds line the river bank.

There are many old pubs and inns on the Thames in the Goring area. This is one of the oldest, the Old Leather Bottle, just outside the village on the way to South Stoke.

Due to the fall in flow of the river, Goring has two locks within a short distance. This is Cleeve Lock *c.*1920.

At the end of the last century there was a timber yard beside the river bridge at Goring, owned by the local builder, Mr Higgs.

Just around the corner from the Goring High Street and the church stood these charming old cottages *c.*1890.

A view of the Goring river bridge and entrance to the lock *c*.1930.

Looking down Goring High Street from the railway bridge *c*.1910.

A closer view of the early Goring river bridge *c*.1890.

Half a mile from Goring Mill stands the enchanting Cleeve Mill. Whilst both still stand, neither are now working mills.

Queen Victoria's Golden Jubilee celebrations on the Recreation Ground in the village of Goring.

As the Thames flows on to Reading we can see the old Whitchurch Bridge in the background *c.*1910.

Pangbourne village as it was at the turn of the century with the River Pang flowing under the old bridge.

The old weir at Pangbourne village, which stretches across the Thames from the Swan Inn, seen on the left.

The great floods of 1894 when the River Thames and the Pang overflowed to inundate the village.

Another view of the horseshoe weir at Pangbourne and a good view of the Swan Inn from across the Thames.

Going up the river at Pangbourne.

A local delivery van in North Street, Pangbourne, at the turn of the century.

The wide expanse of the Thames, at Pangbourne, often called The Stretch but correctly named Shooters Hill.

Pangbourne as it was in the 1950s with a view of the Elephant Hotel, later called the Copper Kettle.

The ancient village of Whitchurch with the charm of the centuries-old Greyhound pub as it was in bygone days.

A charming view of the old ferry as it nestled in by the trees at Whitchurch *c.*1880.

The parish church has always played an important part in the community of the village of Whitchurch.

Another view of the ferry with the old wooden toll bridge in the background, Whitchurch *c*.1885.

This new Whitchurch iron bridge which replaced the wooden one in 1923; note the boats on the right, lined up at The Wharf.

Reflections in the stillness of the Thames at Whitchurch and Pangbourne.

This is the gravel dredger on the Thames at Whitchurch, clearing the channel for the ferry.

This is Streatley's charming nineteenth-century church, although its tower is 500 years old.

One of the old mills which stood at the beginning of the bridge over the Thames, opposite the famous Swan Inn.

Another of the charming views of Streatley Church, seen from across the River Thames.

The main crossroads at Streatley has always been a good focal point of the village because of the old Bull Hotel on the left and the Wells family store on the right.

Streatley High Street has housed many famous people such as Admiral Collins, and Mrs Morrell, who used to own Morrell's Brewery.

This beautiful view of the River Thames shows it wending its way through Streatley and the Goring Gap.

This view taken from Streatley Hill shows the village church and Thames *c.*1920.

As the river wends itself into the valley between the Streatley Hills we have this view as it was in 1930.

Streatley bridge and old weir, as it was around 1910.

Subscribers

B R Aburrow
F L Aburrow
Geoffrey Aburrow
M Aburrow
Alison
W.G.Allen
Robert Auger
Madge Baker
Julie & Arthur Barlow
Peter & Mary Baxter
M F Benjamin
Rosemary Bowyer (USA)
Louise Boylan
Brian Broad
W G & M A Broad
Ulrike Burwood
Joseph Carey
Barbara Carter
Mrs B M Chambers
Mrs B M Chambers
S M Chapple
Mrs K Charlton
L Cohen
John Collis
Phil Coventry
Graham Dore
Jean Dore
John Douce
David Downs
John Easterling
AD Edwards
A D Edwards
M D Eynott
Mr M J Faulkes
Mr Bob Fennell
Mrs C Fostekew
Albret Fryer
Mrs Marion Gale
David Gerken
Mr Philip Gibbins
David L Gillman
Mr D H Grainger

Harry V Jermey
B Hadnam
John Holt
Liz Holt
W J H Illsley
Patricia Jarman
Mr J G Kendall
Harold J King
Mrs Diana Kyle
William Langford
Joan Law
Joan Law
Jean Lovelock
Evangeline MacKenzie
Roland Marks
B A Moulden
Mr L Norriss
Mr P J Nugent
C R Panting
Mr Alan Parsons
S Parsons
S Parsons
E Penfold
Mrs G Potts
R H Read
Mr T B H Rose
Jack Sharpe
G J Smith
A M Taylor
Colleen Thatcher
Evelyn Thomas
W P Vivian
P Walsh
D Ward
Alf Warrick
S Wellenkamp
Mr Derrick West
J Wharton
N Wicks
Mr P Wiggins
Susan Willmott
Mrs N Wilson
Ray Winter
Sheila Wood